A Note to Parents and Teachers

Eyewitness Readers is a compelling new reading programme for children. *Eyewitness* has become the most trusted name in illustrated books and this new series combines the highly visual *Eyewitness* approach with engaging, easy-to-read stories. Each *Eyewitness Reader* is guaranteed to capture a child's interest while developing his or her reading skills, general knowledge and love of reading.

The books are written by leading children's authors and are designed in conjunction with literacy experts, including Cliff Moon M.Ed., Honorary Fellow of the University of Reading. Cliff Moon spent many years as a teacher and teacher educator specializing in reading. He has written more than 140 books for children and teachers and he reviews regularly for teachers' journals.

The four levels of *Eyewitness Readers* are aimed at different reading abilities, enabling you to choose the books that are exactly right for each child.

Level One – Beginning to read
Level Two – Beginning to read alone
Level Three – Reading alone
Level Four – Proficient readers

The "normal" age at which a child begins to read can be anywhere from three to eight years old, so these levels are only general guidelines.

No matter which level you select, you can be sure that you're helping children learn to read, then read to learn!

D0496121

DK

A Dorling Kindersley Book
www.dk.com

Created by Leapfrog Press Ltd

For Dorling Kindersley
Senior Editor Linda Esposito
Managing Art Editor Peter Bailey
US Editor Regina Kahney
Production Josie Alabaster
Picture Researcher Liz Moore
Illustrator Mario Capaldi

Reading Consultant
Cliff Moon M.Ed.

Published in Great Britain by
Dorling Kindersley Limited
9 Henrietta Street
London WC2E 8PS

2 4 6 8 10 9 7 5 3 1

Eyewitness Readers™ is a trademark of
Dorling Kindersley Limited, London.

A CIP catalogue record for this book is
available from the British Library.

ISBN 0-7513-5904-1

Colour reproduction by Colourscan, Singapore
Printed and bound in Belgium by Proost

The publisher would like to thank the following
for their kind permission to reproduce their photographs:
Key: t=top, a=above, b=below, l=left, r=right, c=centre

Ancient Art & Architecture: 4tl, 4bl; Bridgeman Art Library: 10tl;
Camera Press Ltd: 34tl, 34bl, 36-7b; Bruce Coleman Limited: 18bl;
Coloursport: 42tl; Corbis UK Ltd: 19b, 29b; Gerry Cranham: 2, 40-1b, 41tr,
42b, 45tl, 45br; Dorling Kindersley Picture Library: 40tl/Lynton Gardiner:
5bl; Lynton Gardiner/American Museum of Natural History: 9;
Christi Graham/Nick Nicholls/British Museum: 5tr; Bob Langrish: 7tr, 13tr,
17tr, 17cl, 32bl, 46c, 47tr, cr, br; Karl Shone: 46bl; Jerry Young: 10bl, 36bl,
37tr, 46br, 46-7b, 47bl, 39br; AJ Drucker, London 1932, portrait of AF
Tschiffely: 12tl; Mary Evans Picture Library: 8b; Herbert Graf, Wien: 24-5,
27br, 30tl, 30bl; Ronald Grant Archive: 20bl, 21br, 23br, 31;
Houghton's Horses: 44b; Hulton Getty: 23t, 45tr; Image Bank: 20tl;
Kobal Collection: 21tl; Bob Langrish: 17tr, 28tr, 35br; taken from "Red Rum"
by Ivor Herbert, William Luscombe Ltd: 39br; John Slater: 39tra;
Peter Newark's Western Americana: 6bl, br, 7br, 8tl, 8cl;
Only Horses: 37cr, 38bl; Pitkin Pictorials/ Household Cavalry: 36tl;
Popperfoto: 43; Ruth Rogers, Eire: 39trb; John Slater: 39tra;
South American Pictures: 14bl; Telegraph Colour Library: 14tl;
Tony Stone Images: 18tl, 35tr; Topham Picturepoint: 22tl;
Trip/F Good: 33tl; "Tschiffely's Ride",
William Heinemann Ltd/Random House: 12tl, 19tr;
Elisabeth Weiland: 26tl, 27tr, 28bl, 29tr;
Jacket: Only Horses Picture Agency: front cover;
Dorling Kindersley/Bob Langrish: back cover.

Contents